Amazing Grace
ACTIVITY BOOKS

Published in 2021 by
Amazing Grace Activity Books
USA
amazinggraceactivitybooks.com

Copyright © 2021 Amazing Grace Activity Books

All rights reserved. No part of this publication may be reproduced or transmitted in any form or by any means, without permission in writing from the publisher.

As a special thank you for getting this book, we would love to give you a free gift.

Go to our website to get your free downloadable coloring pages!

www.amazinggraceactivitybooks.com

And as you color in your beautiful designs, don't just hide them - go to our facebook group and share them!

www.facebook.com/groups/amzggrace/

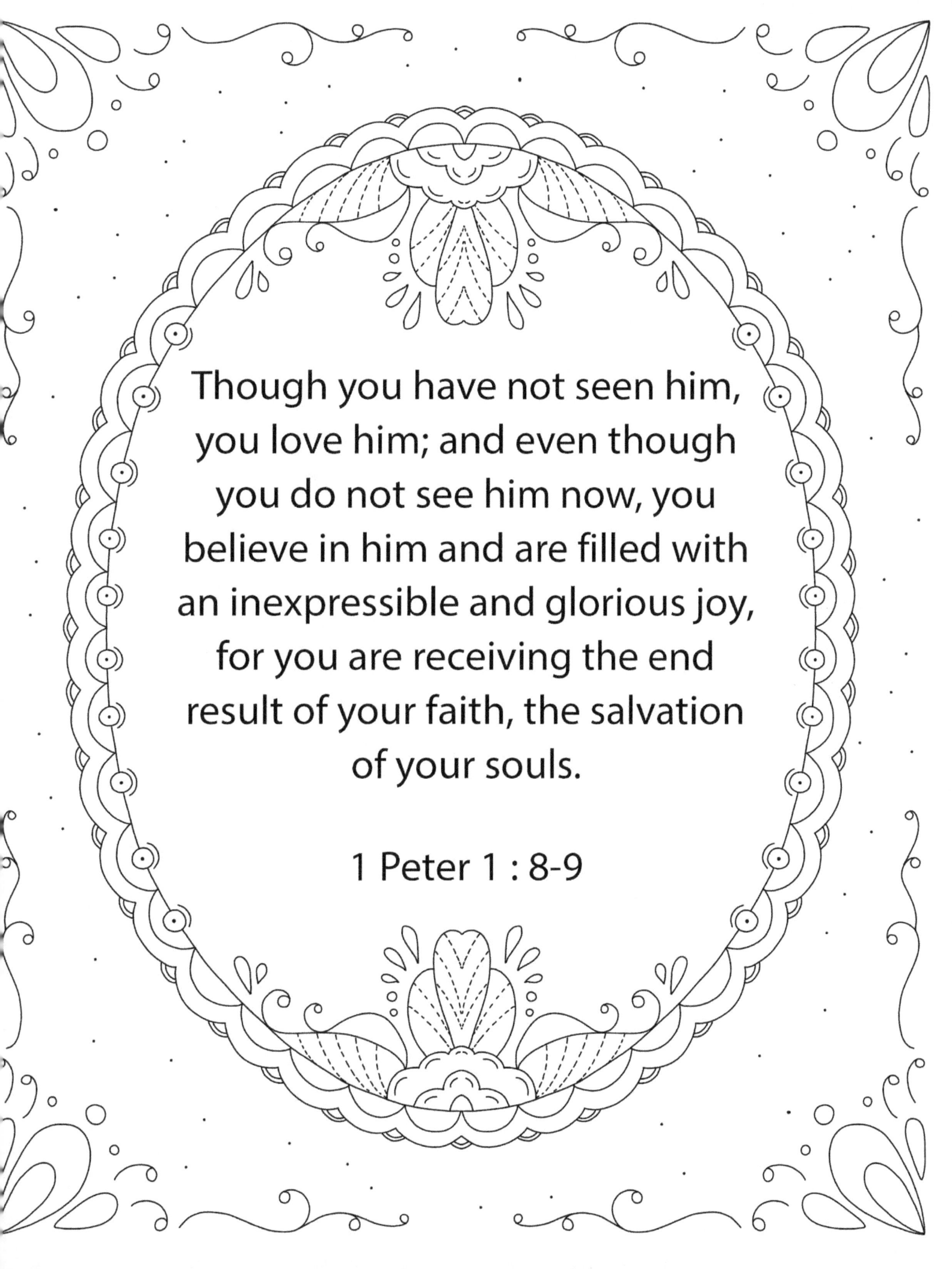

Though you have not seen him, you love him; and even though you do not see him now, you believe in him and are filled with an inexpressible and glorious joy, for you are receiving the end result of your faith, the salvation of your souls.

1 Peter 1 : 8-9

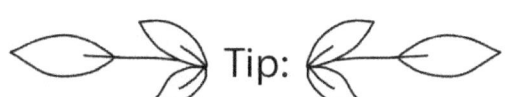 Tip:

This coloring book features single-sided coloring pages to help prevent bleed through if using markers instead of colored pencils. As an extra measure of precaution, you can also put a sheet or two of paper behind the page you are coloring.

Here's how to get the most out of this book:

- Get comfortable.

- Find a clean, quiet, relaxing space.

- Play music, spray your favorite scent, or have your favorite snack or beverage nearby if you want to help set the tone.

- Organize your coloring materials.

- Start coloring and enjoy!

The word of God has a way of being timely and finding us at exactly the right time. With that in mind, you don't have to use this book in order. To help you meditate on a particular verse of choice, you can flip through and find one that you particularly need or that particularly speaks to you in the moment, and color it as a way to relax, have fun, and connect with the words of God you need the most at the time.

Happy coloring!

And the peace of God, which surpasses all understanding, will guard your hearts and your minds in Christ Jesus.

Philippians 4:7

Congrats, you finished! You are quite the talented artist.

Feeling proud of your creations?

Share them in our facebook group:

www.facebook.com/groups/amzggrace/

Amazing Grace
ACTIVITY BOOKS

If you enjoyed using this book as much as we enjoyed making it, please leave a review on the product page on Amazon.

Here are just a few of the other fun, faith filled books we have available on Amazon

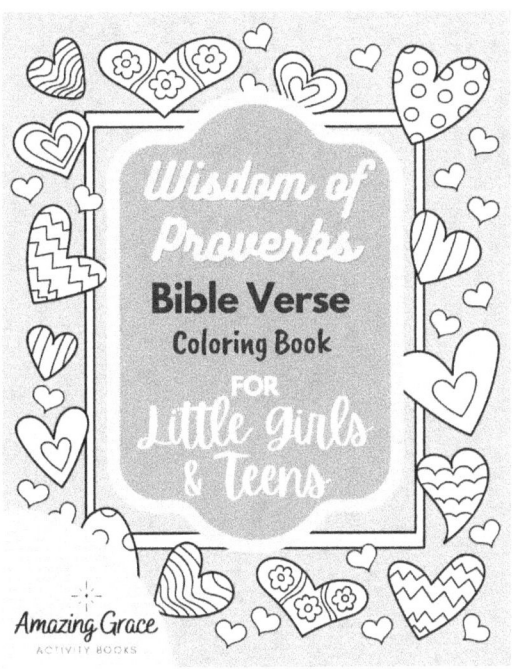